I'll Be in 4th Grade Soon, Right? (...So I Can Start a Band Instrument?)

MILISSA NELSON

ISBN:0-578-58964-8
ISBN-13:978-0-578-58964-0

First Edition: November 2019
Printed in the United States of America
Published by Birch Bark Press
Sartell, MN 56377

DEDICATION

Dedicated to my dad, Elwood Nelson, a true "Music Man".

ACKNOWLEDGMENTS

Thank you to my father, Elwood, for sharing his love of music with me, and our whole family! Once after practicing a piece of jazz music, my youngest daughter told me, "You sounded a little like Grandpa on that one." Truly what I'm always aiming for! Thank you to my mother, Beverly, for reading to me regularly, and for helping me to develop a love of both reading and writing! Thank you to my grandmother, Helen, my parents, Elwood and Beverly, and siblings, Janelle, Jill, Jacqueline, Meredith, Michael, Michelle, and Mark, for patiently allowing me to practice, even when my sound was not exactly pleasant to listen to. Thank you to my husband, Chris, and daughters, Megan and Cora, who sometimes try to watch television or study, while I attempt to build-up an embouchure. Thank you to all of the band directors I have interacted with over the years. Thank you, Mr. Hanson, Mr. Swanson, Mrs. Vedell, Mr. Erikson, Professor Sawchuk, Professor Miles, Professor McMurray, Dr. Bailey, Dr. Caneva, Mr. Zachman, Mr. Huwa, Mr. Olson, and so many others. Thank you for helping to inspire my study of music and the trumpet! Thank you also to Karen Alvstad for permission to use her photos.

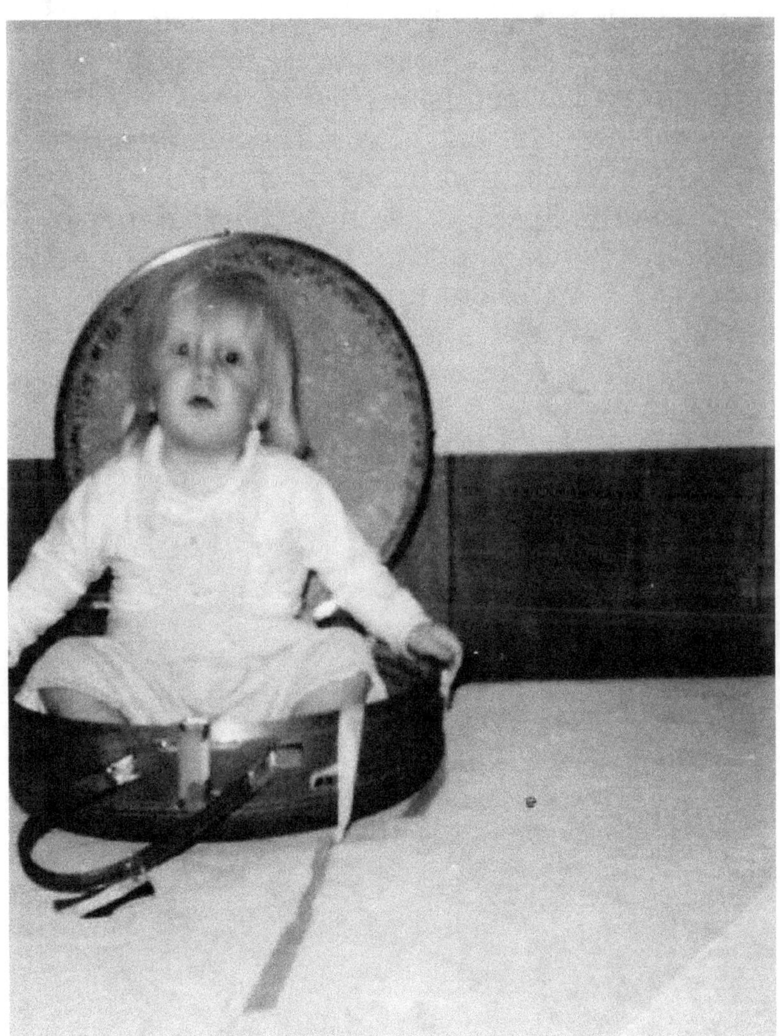

Milissa could not wait to have and operate a band instrument case of her own!

Milissa grew up in a house immersed in music. She lived in Minnesota with her parents, and seven siblings: Janelle, Jill, Jacqueline, Meredith, Michael, Michelle, and Mark. Her dad, Elwood, played trumpet, taught band and choir, and played in a polka band. Her mom, Beverly, loved to listen to classical music. Her six oldest siblings all played band instruments and sang in the choir. Her older brother, Michael, had a stereo, plus, an acoustic and electric guitar. Her little brother, Mark, sang a lot as he moved about the house.

The Nelson Family after having sung in church! Milissa is pictured on the bottom left. She always felt privileged to get to sing with her siblings. She did her best to try and keep up.

Milissa imitated her dad's trumpet sounds with her lips pressed together as she marched down the hallway and participated In a mock parade, created from her own imagination. She sang along with her family members' records and stood in front of Michael's large stereo speakers to do so, because then it felt like she was actually a part of the group. She didn't have the volume turned up very loudly, she knew to be careful, but it made her feel like she was a part of the band, when she was closer to where the sound came from. For songs she didn't already know, she transcribed the words to the vocals, by lifting and replacing the needle on the records, many, many, many, times, until she had them all written down. Milissa could not wait to play in her dad's school band. But…, she was only in 2nd grade.

Milissa with her dad and Michelle!

Milissa's dad!

Another year passed. She kept singing with her sisters and brothers and they even sang together on a telethon show called, ***Jingle Bells***. But still…she was not old enough to join the band. She was only a 3rd grader.

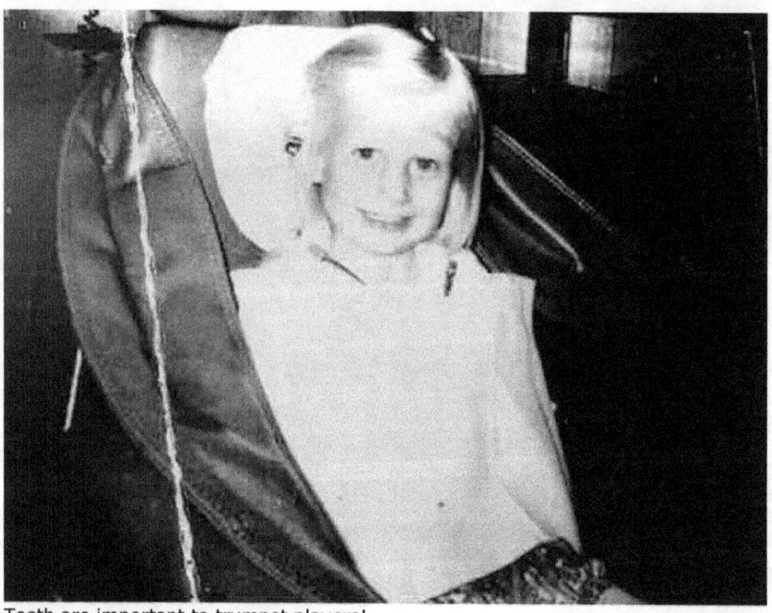

Teeth are important to trumpet players!

She kept herself busy singing along with records to: ***Avalon, You Light Up My Life***, ***Orange Colored Sky, On a Clear Day, Don't It Make My Brown Eyes Blue, Close to You, It's So Easy, Ozzie the Ostrich, My Favorite Things, A Foggy Day, Take Me Home Country Roads,*** and so many other songs. She helped to put on several Thanksgiving and Christmas shows with Michelle and Mark. She took baton lessons with Michelle, and they marched along with their batons and classmates. They twirled down the street to their memorized routine, during the local parades. Her dad led the school marching band in the same parades. She wanted to be in his group and to take part by being in the marching band. Her baton fell on the street a lot, when she tossed it into the air during her routine. That was not supposed to happen. She picked it up quickly and marched onward.

The Christmas Show Team!

Another member of the Christmas Show Team! The fireplace hearth made for a great stage.

Milissa's slightly older sister, Michelle, has always taken such great care of her!

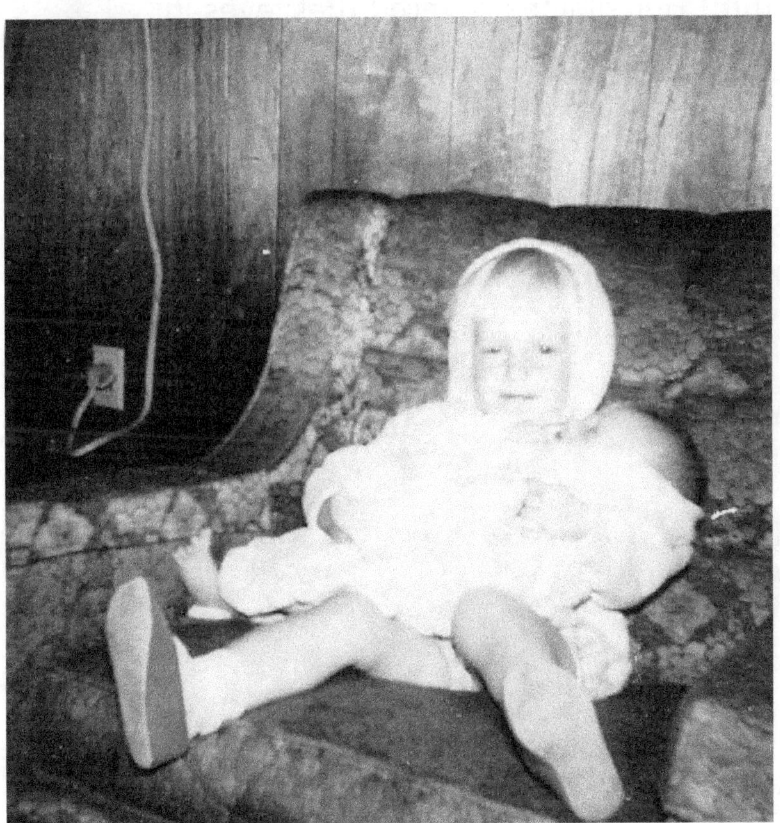

Milissa tapping her toes to some music.

Milissa's dad held a jazz band concert in the high school gym and people were invited to dance to the music. Milissa skipped and skipped and skipped along to the music, and circled the dance floor many times. What fun!! Her siblings covered their eyes in embarrassment, as she passed them frequently, when she traveled around and around the gym.

Milissa's very lovely parents! So fortunate!

All dressed-up and ready to dance and skip! Milissa's dad read the Sunday paper.

At the high school basketball game, her dad directed the pep band. Milissa got to come along. She was treated to *Hot Tamales* and popcorn. She sat by her dad, in the metal bleachers, until just before the B game was over. She helped her dad, and other band members, to set up chairs and stands, and then the A team came out to warm-up. And...once the band started to play...and...all of her older siblings and her dad were busy...she did what she wanted to do. She exited the stage area via the sparkly green steps. (They looked like they had glitter in them!) She passed the girls' locker room, went out the swinging doors to the hallway, and...skipped and skipped and skipped again, all in time to the music. She skipped by the elementary classrooms, the bathrooms and regular student locker area. She paused briefly to look and see if she recognized anyone, in the displayed graduation photos, that lined the upper wall. She happily located a neighbor's senior picture, and skipped on again. In no time at all, she found herself on the opposite side of the gym, where she found the matching sparkly green steps, leading to the stage. This time the steps were near the boys' locker room entrance. She went up the steps and finished her route, as she crossed behind the stage bleachers, and the performing band. After she'd passed by the trombone section, she was reunited with her initial favorite sparkly green steps, yet again. She went down them, exited to the hallway, and started to complete another lap. She'd even felt the music when she'd skipped so close to the band! While the pre-game minutes ticked down, Milissa happily skipped her route, over and over again. She'd listened to **Brandy**, **Ja-Da**, **The Horse**, **Sky High**, **Gonna Fly Now**, **The Muppet Show Theme**, **Hogan's Heroes March**, and **Barrett High's school song (The Minnesota Rouser)**. She returned to stand by her

spot in the bleachers, for ***The Star Spangled Banner***, and no one was the wiser. Her family had been busy after all, and she'd been elusive.
But…, why had the principal of her school, just looked at her so sternly? The music was in her, she'd needed to do something while the band played. She wasn't old enough yet to play an instrument. She waited innocently for halftime, and… planned to skip again, and…she patiently waited one more year to start an instrument.

Games in the gym, viewed from the stage.

Suddenly, Milissa was a 4th grader!! "Hooray, Hooray!!" said Milissa, "Now, I can join the band!!"

Her dad said he had two instruments available at home for her to pick from. He said if she liked one of them, she could even switch to something similar later on, as it became available, but she could start right now on the clarinet, or the trumpet.

"Oh, I will play the TRUMPET!!!!!!!" said Milissa, in an uncharacteristically decisive decision.

Sisters who had seen her cry, rather than pick between the only two possible pairs of shoes that had fit her narrow heels at a shoe store, were simply shocked by her certainty!

Band girl, with some fashion challenges, who always needed to hem or cuff her new pants. Milissa posed before she had begun alterations.

She joined the 4th grade band and practiced every day! After too much practice had caused her German Shepherd, Lady, to howl, and made Lady sound like she was singing along, but with a rather ear piercing singing voice, Milissa's grandma, who had also patiently listened to Milissa's many daily trumpet practice sessions, said, "That's enough now."

Then, they opened the front door, to let Lady outside. After that, Milissa tried to make sure her dog, Lady, was already outdoors, when she practiced. She didn't want to hurt Lady's ears. It was also harder for Milissa to hear if her trumpet pitches were correct, when Lady participated.

Milissa collected weekly *Tootsie Roll* rewards at school for completed practice minutes. Milissa loved candy! It was a good motivator for her. In a large family like hers, candy did not stick around for very long.

Milissa's dog, Lady, who liked her more, when she wasn't playing the trumpet!

Since Milissa went to a K-12, she joined the high school band in 6th grade! She now took part in parades and in pep band. This curtailed her pre-game and halftime hallway skipping, but...now she got into the basketball games for free! And...in the summer, she also received a coupon for a free P.T.S.O. (Parent/Teacher/Student Organization) meal at the food stand after the parade! Those barbecues (Sloppy Joes) were the best!

20 lbs Hamb
2 lg cans tomato
Ketchup. 1 Sm bottle Soup
1 Sm jar - dried onion
1 Bag B. Sugar
20 doz buns -

The recipe!

She still practiced her lesson book at home, and
played the exercises out of it, for weekly band lessons
at school. Also, when her older siblings were home,
she recruited them to play the pieces they now had in
common. They started and stopped frequently, and
switched from piece to piece, as Milissa struggled with
the music. Her older siblings said after each piece, "I
thought you said you knew that one."

"Still working on it," said Milissa, undeterred and
happily.

Thanks to listening to her more skilled siblings play
the music, now she really knew what the pieces
should sound like. It had been hard to figure out the
counting on her own. She went back to practicing with
new insights. Milissa's skills increased and she loved
to play in the band.

Milissa's Barrett High School parade shirt! This was worn with white pants or white jeans. The band stayed cool in the heat this way!

Barrett's K-12 (School District #262)

When Milissa was in 7th grade, the school band took part in ***The World's Largest Marching Band*** in Minneapolis. Meredith Willson, who wrote the book, music, and lyrics to ***The Music Man***, conducted the large ensemble, on ***Seventy-Six Trombones***. Dr. Frank Bencriscutto, Director of Bands at the University of Minnesota, was visible from an elevated bucket, atop an aerial ladder of a fire truck, in the front of the very long and large group. They lined up alphabetically, so near the front, the Barrett band marched close to the Elmore band, another small town, whose members told Milissa that Vice-President Walter Mondale was from their hometown. The University of Minnesota Band took part too. They were excellent! Milissa played several songs with the large group. She probably could've stood to have had the skills to play them better, but...she did her best. It was still fun! She also received a T-shirt that told about breaking the World Record!

She's older, but she still has her shirt!

The Old Setters' Days Parade on Main Street in Barrett.

Milissa continued to play in the school band and sing in the choir. She took part in large group and small solo and ensemble contests with the band and choir. She played in front of judges (called adjudicators) and was given verbal and written advice on how to improve. She started playing solos in band pieces. She found it scary, but really fun. She tried to make the most musical sounding tones that she could on her trumpet. Band was her favorite class! She disliked it when a non-musical substitute filled in, who didn't feel comfortable conducting, and therefore, let them have a study period. Although, she should have just been grateful that the substitute was willing to be there, and she did usually benefit from the study period. Milissa was only disappointed, because she just really wanted to play every day! She loved to play the trumpet!

Dressed-up for a Christmas Concert!

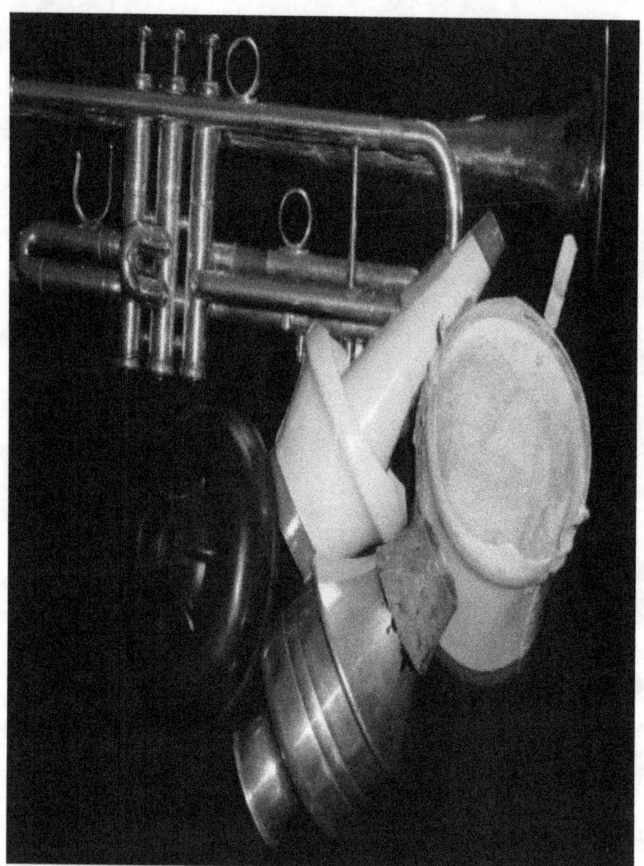

Who wouldn't want to play a trumpet?! Adding a mute, changes the sound. Pictured here: a Cup Mute, Harmon Mute, Bucket Mute and a Plunger Mute.

Milissa with a portion of her family at Parents' Night for a basketball game!
You can see the stage behind them, where Milissa could make half of an entire skip
lap happen, before she had been old enough to take part, as a member of the band.
Here she was a member of the girls' basketball team! That meant she could once
again, listen and move along to the beat of the pep songs, at least part of the
time. Also, she could still play with the pep band for the boys' games! She was able
to increase her lung power for trumpet, by running in basketball practice and games.

Milissa sat in and played a set of three polkas with her dad's band on Sundays, when they played at a supper club, and she also joined them at the East Ottertail County Fair. Milissa loved to play her trumpet! Her dad also taught her to play, from memory, ***The Peanuts Polka, The Ottertail Polka, and Don't Cry, My Anna!***

The Blue Knights at the Otter Supper Club in Ottertail, MN.

Milissa's family moved to Colorado. They were now in a big town. Boulder had two large high schools! She had played in a grade 6-12 band, sung in a similar sized choir, surely she could no longer take part. She came from Barrett, a town of 388 people, now there were over 650 students in her grade level at Boulder High. The groups at the big school would be too advanced, she thought.

Milissa's parents said, "You'll do great. Give it a try!"

Milissa could now hike! Here she was in the foothills above Boulder, where she often hiked with family!

Milissa's brother, Mark, played percussion instruments for Boulder High too! He was younger, so he played with Boulder High for three years! The sun is much closer in Colorado, so...sunglasses!

Milissa showed up for the choir, found an empty spot on the riser, as school had already been in session for a few days, and blended in. When choir class started, the choir director paused, looked at her, and said, "...You're new!"

"Yes," said Milissa.

"Welcome, sing with us. We're glad you're here!" said the director.

This is why practicing trumpet in her Barrett bedroom had made it harder for others to hear the television or sometimes just their own conversations. Both lovely and not so lovely sounds soared over the rafters or between the logs, and were shared with anyone who was home. Milissa says she should really thank her family the most, for putting up with all of her practice time over the years. She also learned to put a mute in, to practice more quietly, when she lived in Boulder.

When Milissa showed up for band, the group was getting ready to head out to the football field.

"Is this the concert band?" said Milissa, who was confused, because that is what she had signed-up for at registration.

"Yes, but not for another month or so," said the band director, who explained that the group had gone to a camp in the mountains during the summer, to learn the field show. "Until football season is over, we march. What part did you play at your old school?" the director asked.

"First," said Milissa. The director handed her a second part without even an audition, as he already had the first parts covered.

"You'll be fine," he said, sensing her apprehension as he pointed to an empty spot for her to stand in. "We have a spot to fill in that row. Just stay between the two marchers on either side of you."

She did her best and got busy memorizing the 2nd trumpet part to **Autumn Leaves** and the school song, **Boulder High Loyalty**. The 2nd part was not as easy to memorize as the melody would have been. She eventually played concert music and took part in large and small group contest again. She played a trumpet solo and an exchange student from England, who was also new, offered to accompany her on the piano for the contest. His name was Charles and he had bright red hair, but what Milissa appreciated most about him, was his kindness. He was also a good pianist.

Growing up in the country though, had afforded certain advantages. The next door neighbors were not close enough to hear Milissa's initial trumpet sounds. Although, on a clear and calm day, with the windows open, the sound did bounce off of the lake water a little. She could also, with some consideration given to her family, practice at night. In Boulder, she worked harder to practice during daylight hours.

No matter where Milissa went to school, the letters looked the same.

The time came for Milissa to apply to colleges to continue her study of music. With the help of her counselor, she applied to several schools, mostly smaller ones. She also applied to the University of Colorado College of Music, with little hope of being accepted. After all, she was playing the 2nd trumpet part now, and she knew there was a required audition. That scared her. The smaller schools hadn't needed one.

She ate lunch with a girl she'd met as a friend of a friend from history class. Her name was Amy, and Milissa learned that she took piano lessons. She asked Amy to accompany her on a solo trumpet piece for the audition. Milissa played **Presto** by Georg Phillip Telemann, and Amy, her new friend, even offered her home to practice at. That was cool, because Amy had a piano, and lived in the foothills, Sugar Loaf Canyon, to be exact. It was pretty up there.

Milissa went to the audition...and...survived...and...was told that day...that she'd been accepted!! Shocked!! Surprised!! She made new plans to attend CU-Boulder. She graduated from Boulder High School, where she sang, **Stand by Me**, with the senior choir members during the ceremony, and made more plans.

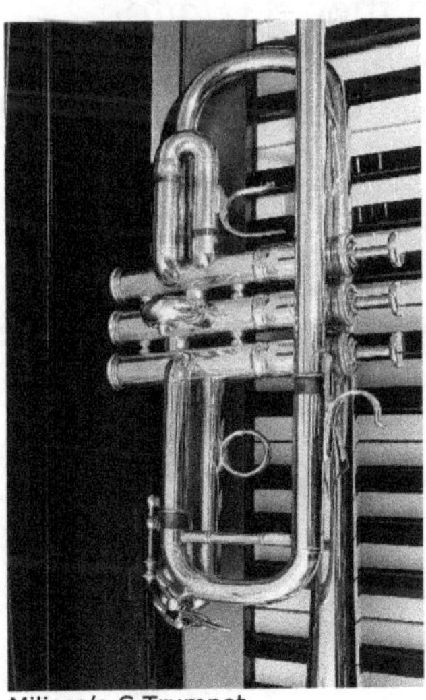

Milissa's C Trumpet.

Milissa practiced trumpet over the summer. She had been known to take the summers mostly off. Who doesn't love a good break? Later on, she arrived a little timidly for orientation. They told her as a music education major, that she'd have to be in the marching band for two years. She'd not planned on that. She liked concert band better. Her parents had just purchased a Maynard Ferguson model, *Holton* brand trumpet, for Milissa, the previous fall. It had snowed on her and on her nice, new, silver trumpet during football games at Boulder High, and she'd only marched in formations for one year. Previous to that, she'd only known street marching. But...she signed-up. What else could she do? Two years were required for her major. And...although there were three rehearsals a day, the week before school started, which required her to arrive a week ahead of all the other freshman,...she ~~liked~~ LOVED it!! She happily continued to earn the one credit that came with having taken a semester of marching band, for four years straight!

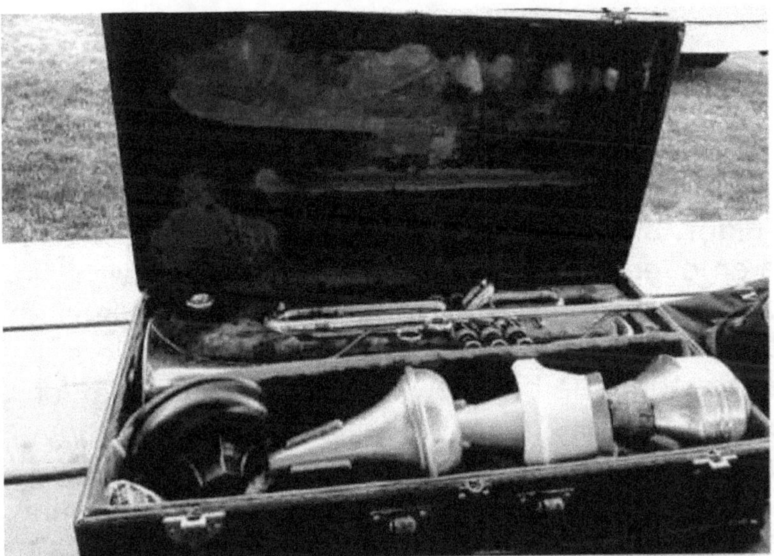

Milissa's trumpet case at a jazz band concert. Mutes took up all of the extra room. Here you can see what a Straight Mute looks like. It is next to the easy to identify, Plunger Mute.

For University of Colorado Golden Buffalo Marching Band members, there was something fun to do almost every night, after the three daily rehearsals, too. Milissa enjoyed an ice cream social, a bonfire with hayrides, a hike to look at stars, viewed from Flagstaff Mountain, and a picnic dinner. By the time University classes started, she had new friends. The first day of classes, did not feel like a first day. She was already comfortable. Of all of the classes she enrolled in, it could've easily required the biggest time commitment. Milissa didn't mind though, in fact she loved being a part of the marching band!

Milissa loved the cowboy hat! The most comfortable band hat she'd ever worn! This was a trying on the uniform pose. Technically, the hat should be pushed down and cover her hair, as much as possible, to ensure all band members looked alike. She encountered new words, such as: gauntlets, fringe, and bow tie!

Milissa took part in making pictures and shapes on Farrand and Folsom Fields, and played such fun marching music. The band formed the word, *Colorado*, in cursive and made a Buffalo shape on the field. The band members, in the tail, marched back and forth to move it, as the entire band played the fight songs. The band traveled to an "away" game without additional expenses for Milissa. It was a required part of the class, so the University and the Big 8 Conference funds, paid for it.

At a meal after rehearsal for the Orange Bowl Parade and Game!

Hanging out with her favorite trumpet player! Milissa says her dad is often humming, singing, or playing trumpet. She loves listening and singing along with him to Big Band Music in the car. He often had the whole family harmonizing as they traveled down the road in their light green station wagon. A good way to keep them all occupied on a long drive.

Milissa took more trumpet lessons at the University, some from a talented graduate student, and many more from the skilled trumpet studio teacher. She took part in Symphonic Band, Concert Band, The Wednesday Night Band, The University of Colorado Basketball Pep Band, Jazz Band II, The Kappa Kappa Psi National Honorary Band Fraternity Jazz Band, and a brass quintet. She played in a small group for a campus-wide music day. The football team was successful, so she played trumpet in the Golden Buffalo Marching Band at the Freedom Bowl, the Orange Bowl (twice), the Blockbuster Bowl, and the Fiesta Bowl (all without additional expenses). She traveled for free. She went to Disneyland, Universal Studios, Alligator Alley, the ocean, and a rodeo, all because she was a member of the band. She also performed at Boettcher Concert Hall in Denver as part of a multi-part trumpet ensemble during a Colorado Symphony Concert.

She was asked to fill-in an empty marching band spot, when an enrolled member could not attend, for bowl games, even after she graduated, as she still lived in Boulder!

Folsom Field, made out of ocean sand! Can you see the goal posts?

Milissa graduated, taught, and worked a variety of music jobs. She played trumpet and sang, by choice, with several community groups. She continued to play trumpet with her dad too, and sing with her family. Making music was something she absolutely loved to do!

Milissa's Music Education tassel was light pink!

Milissa graduated with a Bachelor of Music Education degree!

Milissa will never regret starting an instrument and hopes that you will give one a try too!!

About the Author: Milissa Nelson has loved music ever since she can remember. She has made music with her family since she was small. She lives in Minnesota with her husband and two daughters, who while they chose orchestra instruments over the band ones, also love music!

Also by Milissa Nelson - Seasons of Raina, 2013 and Off Track, 2016